Patterns at the Museum

Tracey Steffora

Heinemann Library
Chicago, Illinois

www.capstonepub.com
Visit our website to find out more information about Heinemann-Raintree books.

To order:

☎ Phone 800-747-4992
Visit www.capstonepub.com to browse our catalog and order online.

Edited by Rebecca Rissman, Tracey Steffora, and Catherine Veitch
Designed by Joanna Hinton-Malivoire
Picture research by Elizabeth Alexander
Production by Victoria Fitzgerald
Originated by Capstone Global Library Ltd

Library of Congress Cataloging-in-Publication Data
Steffora, Tracey.
Patterns at the museum / Tracey Steffora.
p. cm.—(Math around us)
Includes bibliographical references and index.
ISBN 978-1-4329-4923-5 (hc)—ISBN 978-1-4329-4931-0 (pb) 1. Pattern perception—Juvenile literature. I. Title.
BF294.S74 2011
152.14'23—dc22 2010030756

Acknowledgments
Alamy: dave jepson, 22, David Rowland, 8, eddie linssen, 9, 23 top, FinnbarrWebster, 17, 23 bottom, First Light, Cover, 7, imagebroker, Back Cover, 10, Joe Vogan, 13, Martin Thomas Photography, 5, mauritius images GmbH, 11, Oliver Knight, 15, 23 middle, Rolf Adlercreutz, 6, Urbanmyth, 20, 21 right, 21 left, World Pictures, 21 middle; Getty Images Inc.: Dan Forer, 19; iStockphoto: visionchina, 4

We would like to thank Nancy Harris, Dee Reid, and Diana Bentley for their assistance in the preparation of this book.

Printed in the United States 5685

Contents

At the Museum

Look around the museum.

Patterns are everywhere.

Lines

Lines can make a pattern.

The lines on these stairs make
a pattern.

Shapes

Shapes can make a pattern.

The shapes on this armor make
a pattern.

Colors

Colors can make a pattern.

The colors on this boat make a pattern.

Find the Pattern

A pattern can go from small to large.

Can you see a pattern in these tiles?

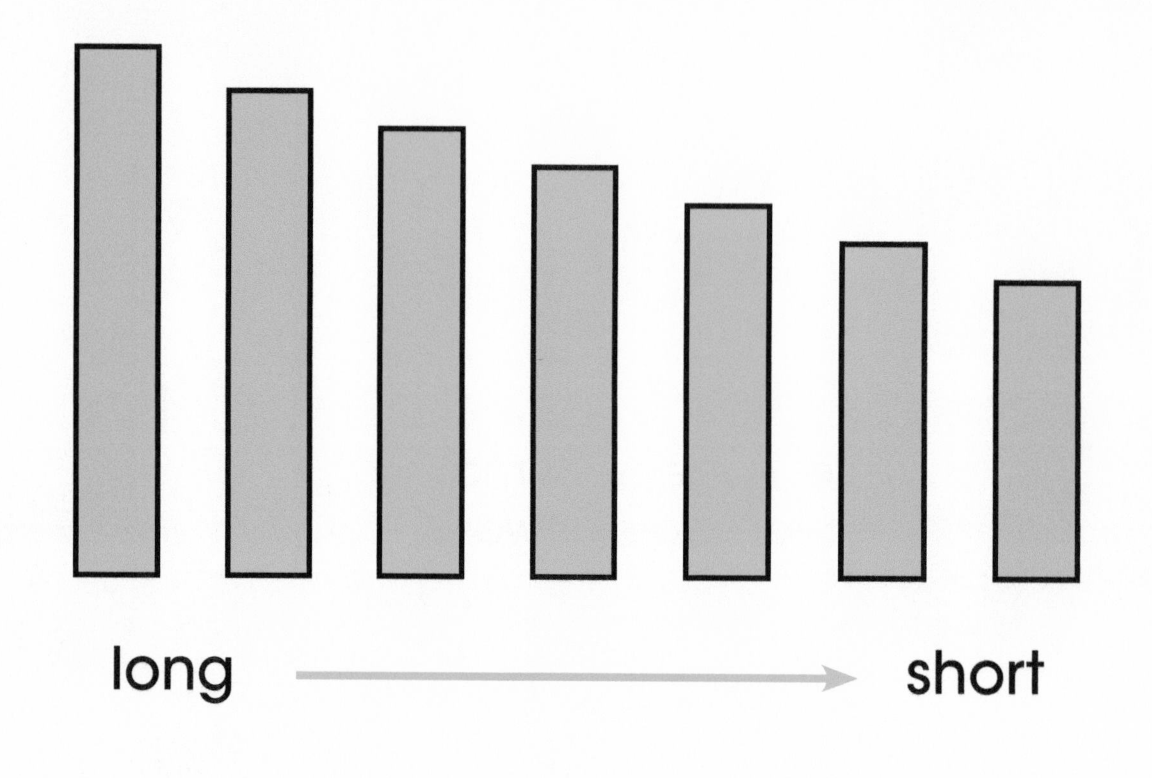

A pattern can go from long to short.

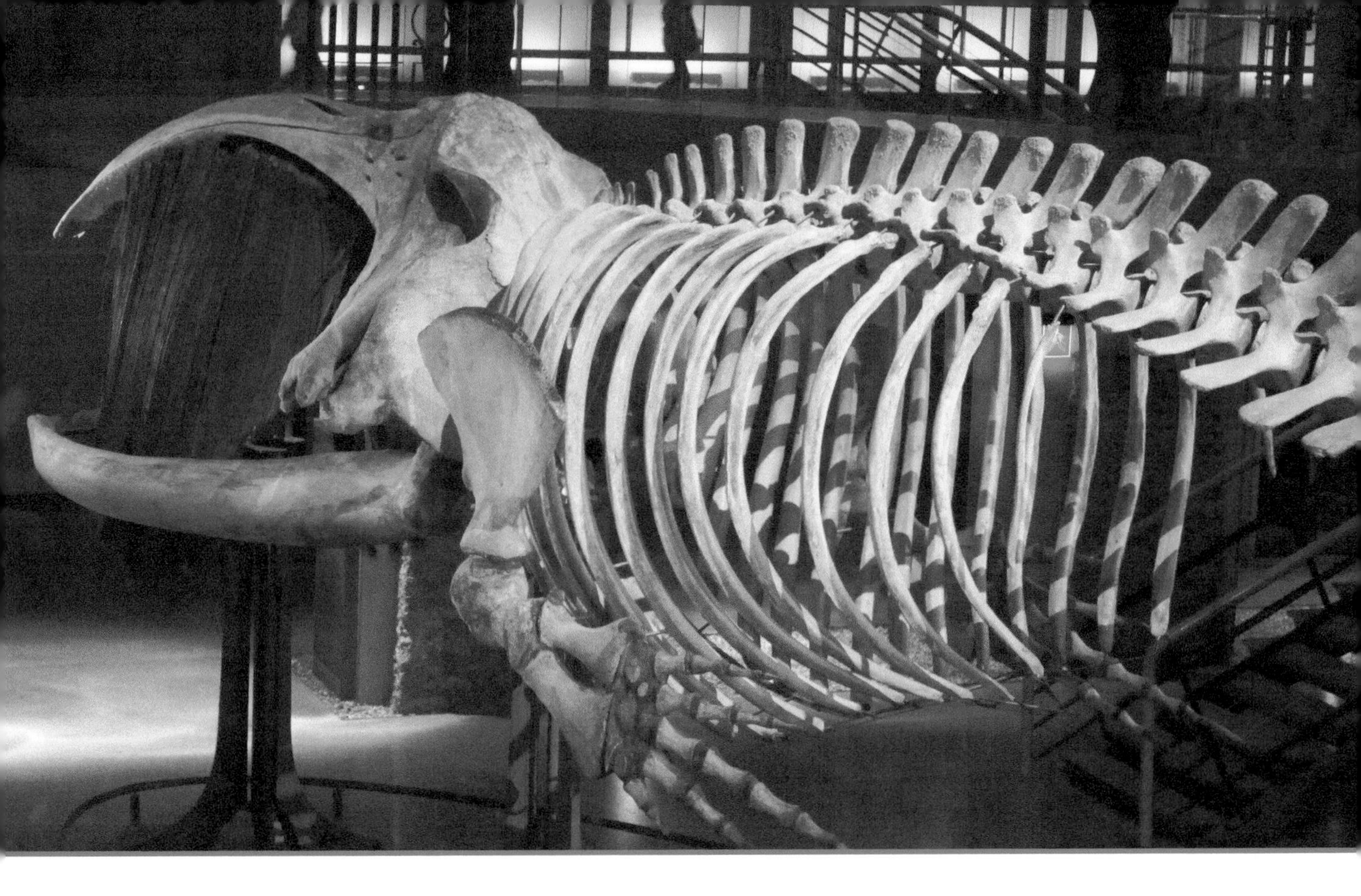

Can you see a pattern in
these bones?

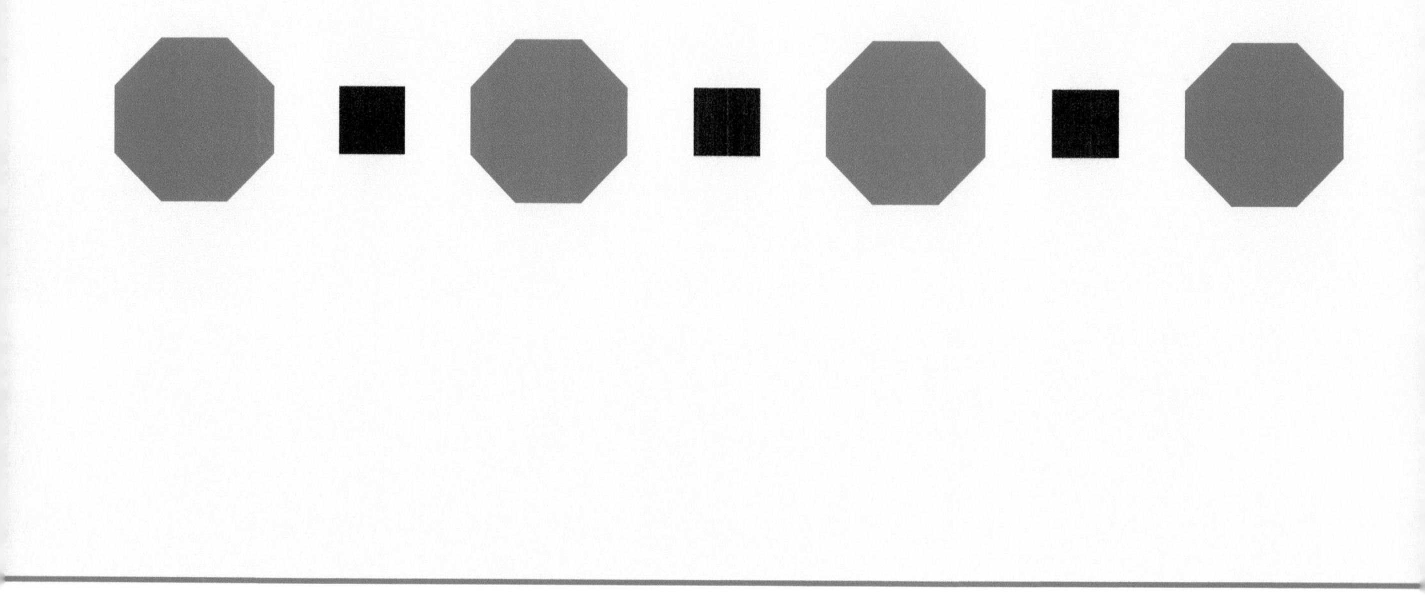

A pattern can repeat.

Can you see a pattern on this floor?

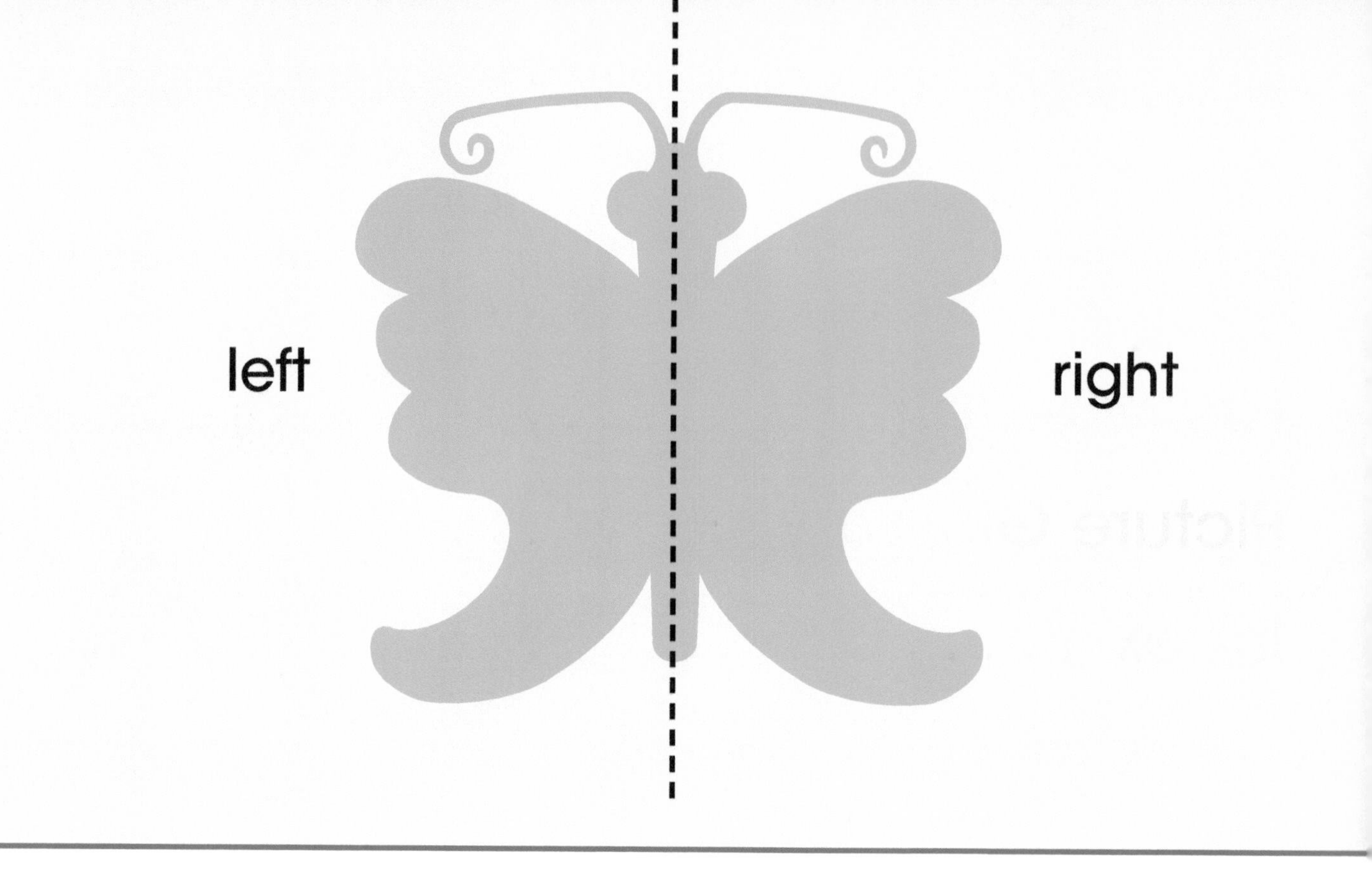

A pattern can match on the left and the right.

Can you see a pattern with these lions?

Look for a pattern in these windows.

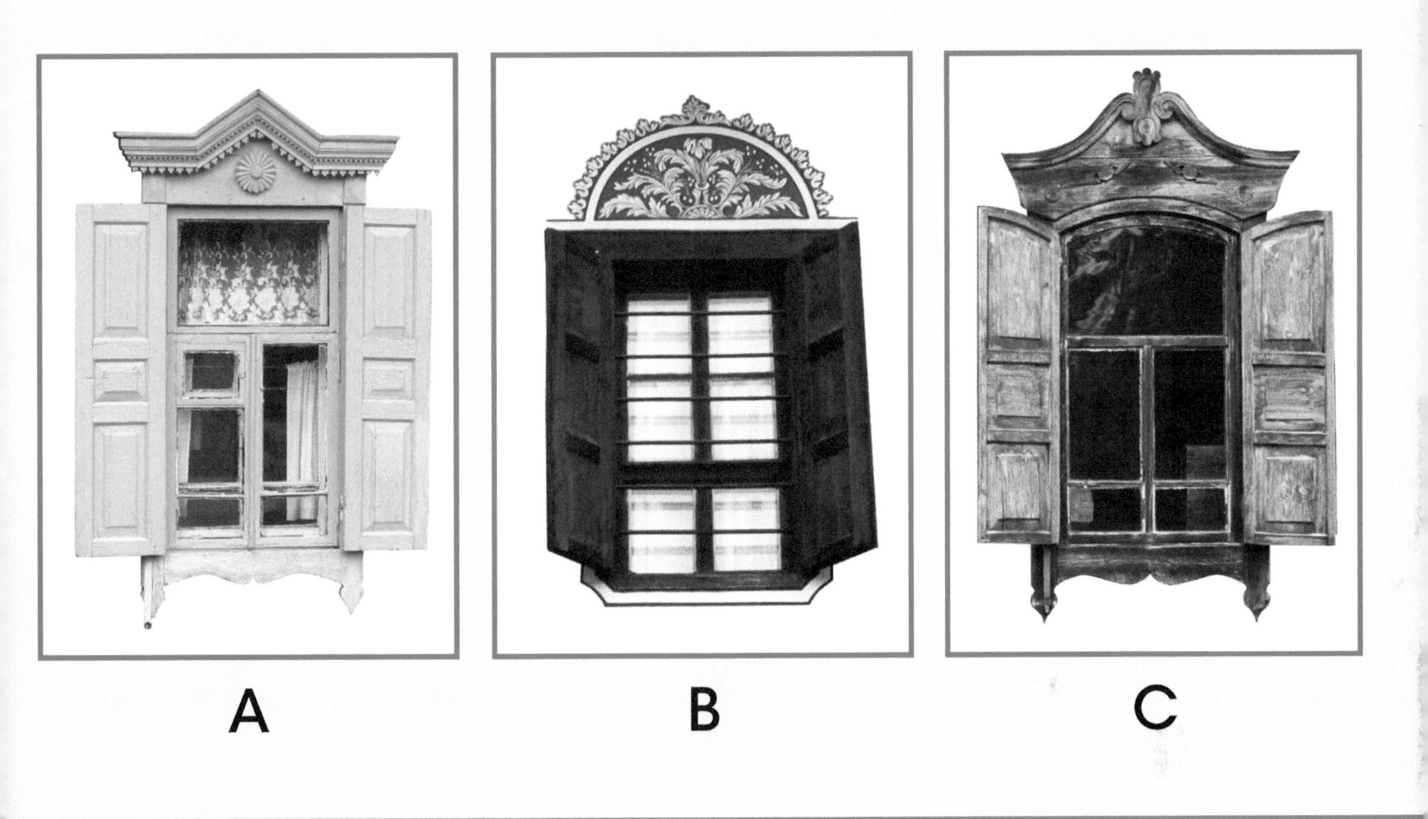

Which one comes next?

How many patterns can you find?

Picture Glossary

armor a metal covering that protects the body in battle

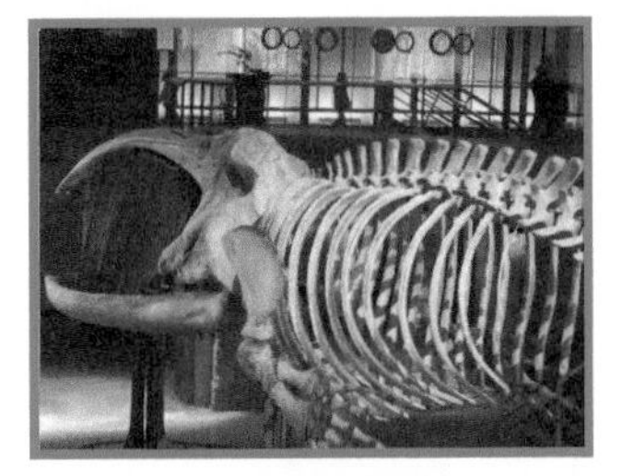

bone a part of the body that forms the skeleton

tile a piece of material used to cover floors or walls

Index

Notes to Parents and Teachers

Before reading

When observing patterns, children are dealing with objects that have a relationship to each other. They are required to respond in a logical way to what they see. Provide children with sets of objects (blocks, beads, coins, leaves) and encourage them to order the objects in different ways (e.g. biggest to smallest, smallest to biggest). Discuss how putting things in order is a type of pattern.

After reading

Review the different types of patterns found in the text. With children, go on a pattern hunt in your school or local environment. Take along a digital camera to record what you find. Print out the photos and sort them with children (e.g., patterns that use lines, colors, shapes). You might then choose to use them in constructing a book.